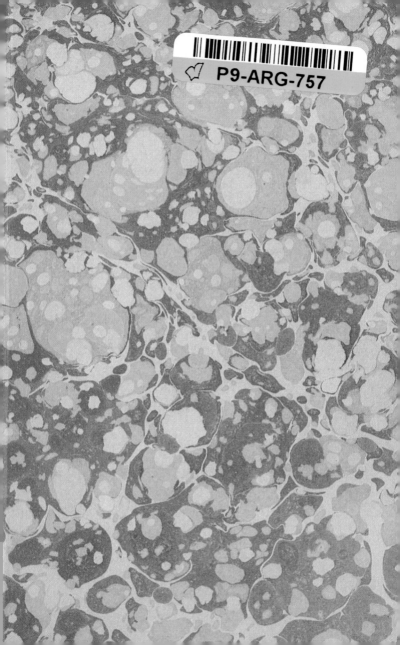

A VOICE WITHIN
THREE WOMEN POETS

A VOICE WITHIN
Three Women Poets

Elizabeth Barrett Browning
Emily Dickinson
Christina Rossetti

Selected with introductions by
Geoffrey Moore and Peter Porter

AURUM PRESS

. . . there's a voice within
That weeps . . . as thou must sing . . . alone, aloof

Elizabeth Barrett Browning, *Sonnets from the Portuguese*

This collection first published 1993 by Aurum Press Limited,
10 Museum Street, London WC1A 1JS

Barrett Browning selection and introduction copyright © 1992 by Peter Porter
Dickinson selection and introduction copyright © 1986 by Geoffrey Moore
Rossetti selection and introduction copyright © 1986 by Peter Porter

A catalogue record for this book is available from the British Library

ISBN 1 85410 262 1

1 3 5 7 9 10 8 6 4 2
1994   1996   1997   1995   1993

Picture research by Juliet Brightmore

Printed in Hong Kong by Imago

CONTENTS

CHRISTINA ROSSETTI

ELIZABETH
BARRETT BROWNING

Elizabeth
Barrett Browning

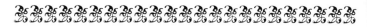

INTRODUCTION

Literature abounds in reputations that continue unfaded though the works which made them are no longer current. Such would be the case with Byron if his letters, a handful of lyrics and *Don Juan* were not still admired. Life has replaced art; the biography excites us while much of the poetry is ignored. Elizabeth Barrett Browning is an unhappy example of public familiarity hardly going beyond her name, other than a few half-remembered romantic details of her elopement, exile and early death. There is a second reason for this effacement – she married one of the greatest poets in the English language, Robert Browning. When they first met, she was the lionized author, one of the most celebrated poets of the early Victorian period. He was a young and unread beginner. At the time of her death in 1861 she was still the better-known of the two. Robert lived on until 1889 and became, after Tennyson, the premier poet of the century. Today he is an immortal, the Father of Modernism, while Elizabeth Barrett's poetry is largely unpublished and unread.

Yet her fame is potent enough in two directions – in romantic legend and through feminism. The first was given currency in a play of the 1930s which became one of the box-office hits of all time – Rudolf Besier's *The Barretts of Wimpole Street*. Here the story of the robust Robert's wooing of the valetudinarian Elizabeth was turned into a triumph of love over parental opposition. The reality was very different, of course, but the legend has sufficient truth in it to make Elizabeth's deliverance from her Wimpole Street sickbed, to begin a new and vigorous existence in Tuscany, a true-life romance. What the play could only hint at was Elizabeth's commanding intelligence, and the originality of her mind. She read Greek and Latin, was absorbed in politics and had an understanding of the social system of her day unique among English women poets. At the same time, her championing of Italian independence (see *Casa Guidi Windows*) was as practical as it was generous.

Feminism has esteemed Elizabeth largely for extra-literary reasons. Her long verse narrative *Aurora Leigh* is undoubtedly a feminist tract, but like all original writers Elizabeth could see more than one side of any case, and this remarkable tale of a woman poet championing a working-class girl who is wronged by an upper-class lover is ironic in its presentation of the need for female liberation. But her scorn for masculine patronage is real: 'How arrogant men are! Even philanthropists/ Who try to take a wife up in the way/ They put down a subscription cheque.' What fits in less well with feminism is her piety, her deep-seated familiarity with the Bible, the works of the Fathers and the early Christian poets. 'God' is probably the most frequently encountered word in her poetry.

Elizabeth Barrett was a copious poet. She even produced an imitation epic *The Battle of Marathon* before she was fifteen. Throughout her life her models were the Greek and Latin classics and the English poets of the Jacobean age and the eighteenth century. Each of her poems is a well-made artefact, and, it must be admitted, many show signs of her laborious craftsmanship. The originality of her vision develops as she faces the reality of the Victorian world she was able to observe from her privileged position. She does not exhibit those touches we can call 'feminine', as Christina Rossetti and, to a far greater extent, Emily Dickinson do. She can strike with great force: nobody summed up the shock of Napoleon as potently as she did in one line in her poem 'Crowned and Buried' – 'And kings crept out again to feel the sun'. Her lyrics are often finely honed and delightfully light – namely 'The Sea-Mew' and 'The Lady's Yes'. Nevertheless, she is usually serious and often sententious, but always liberal of attitude and wonderfully free of vanity. In *Aurora Leigh* she writes, 'For me, I wrote/ False poems, like the rest, and thought them true/ Because myself was true in writing them.' Her diction is unexpectedly modern – she uses words such as 'teens', 'archetype' and 'inflatus' without embarrassment.

Elizabeth was the eldest child of Edward Moulton Barrett, whose wealth derived originally from plantations in Jamaica. She was born in 1806 in the North of England and became the famous invalid of Wimpole Street only after serious illness in early womanhood. Her Tuscan life with Robert Browning was largely happy, despite poor health complicated by miscarriages, but the Italian heat and the rigours of travelling to England and throughout the Continent wore her out. After her death, Robert Browning never again visited Florence and testified, in poem after poem, to his devotion to her memory and to the fierce intellectual spirit which had inhabited so slight and sickly a frame.

Because her finest poems tend to be overlong, I have made several radical shortenings in producing this selection without, I believe, damaging the works concerned; but a full account of my editing in each case is given on page 60. The following pages offer an essence of an unfairly neglected poet whose nature was as realistic as it was passionate. As she wrote in *Sonnets from the Portuguese*, 'God's gifts put man's best dreams to shame.' Her own gifts deserve to be more plainly on view.

From
SONNETS FROM THE PORTUGUESE

Suite of Sonnets

Unlike are we, unlike, O princely Heart!
Unlike our uses and our destinies.
Our ministering two angels look surprise
On one another, as they strike athwart
Their wings in passing. Thou, bethink thee, art
A guest for queens to social pageantries,
With gages from a hundred brighter eyes
Than tears even can make mine, to play thy part
Of chief musician. What hast *thou* to do
With looking from the lattice-lights at me,
A poor, tired, wandering singer, . . . singing
      through
The dark, and leaning up a cypress tree?
The chrism is on thine head, – on mine, the dew, –
And Death must dig the level where these agree.

Thou hast thy calling to some palace-floor,
Most gracious singer of high poems! where
The dancers will break footing, from the care
Of watching up thy pregnant lips for more.
And dost thou lift this house's latch too poor
For hand of thine? and canst thou think and bear
To let thy music drop here unaware
In folds of golden fulness at my door?
Look up and see the casement broken in,
The bats and owlets builders in the roof!
My cricket chirps against thy mandolin.
Hush, call no echo up in further proof
Of desolation! there's a voice within
That weeps . . . as thou must sing . . . alone, aloof.

I lift my heavy heart up solemnly,
As once Electra her sepulchral urn,
And, looking in thine eyes, I overturn
The ashes at thy feet. Behold and see
What a great heap of grief lay hid in me,
And how the red wild sparkles dimly burn
Through the ashen greyness. If thy foot in scorn

Could tread them out to darkness utterly,
It might be well perhaps. But if instead
Thou wait beside me for the wind to blow
The grey dust up, . . . those laurels on thine head,
O my Belovèd, will not shield thee so,
That none of all the fires shall scorch and shred
The hair beneath. Stand further off then! go.

Yet, love, mere love, is beautiful indeed
And worthy of acceptation. Fire is bright,
Let temple burn, or flax. An equal light
Leaps in the flame from cedar-plank or weed.
And love is fire. And when I say at need
I love thee . . . mark! . . . *I love thee* – in thy sight
I stand transfigured, glorified aright,
With conscience of the new rays that proceed
Out of my face toward thine. There's nothing low
In love, when love the lowest: meanest creatures
Who love God, God accepts while loving so.
And what I *feel*, across the inferior features
Of what I *am*, doth flash itself, and show
How that great work of Love enhances Nature's.

And wilt thou have me fashion into speech
The love I bear thee, finding words enough,
And hold the torch out, while the winds are rough
Between our faces, to cast light on each? –
I drop it at thy feet. I cannot teach
My hand to hold my spirit so far off
From myself . . . me . . . that I should bring thee
　　　proof
In words, of love hid in me out of reach.
Nay, let the silence of my womanhood
Commend my woman-love to thy belief, –
Seeing that I stand unwon, however wooed,
And rend the garment of my life, in brief,
By a most dauntless, voiceless fortitude,
Lest one touch of this heart convey its grief.

If thou must love me, let it be for nought
Except for love's sake only. Do not say
'I love her for her smile . . . her look . . . her way
Of speaking gently, . . . for a trick of thought
That falls in well with mine, and certes brought
A sense of pleasant ease on such a day' –
For these things in themselves, Belovèd, may
Be changed, or change for thee, – and love, so
　　　wrought

May be unwrought so. Neither love me for
Thine own dear pity's wiping my cheeks dry, –
A creature might forget to weep, who bore
Thy comfort long, and lose thy love thereby!
But love me for love's sake, that evermore
Thou may'st love on, through love's eternity.

Say over again, and yet once over again,
That thou dost love me. Though the word repeated
Should seem 'a cuckoo-song,' as thou dost treat it,
Remember, never to the hill or plain,
Valley and wood, without her cuckoo-strain
Comes the fresh Spring in all her green completed.
Belovèd, I, amid the darkness greeted
By a doubtful spirit-voice, in that doubt's pain
Cry, . . . 'Speak once more . . . thou lovest!' Who
    can fear
Too many stars, though each in heaven shall roll, –
Too many flowers, though each shall crown the
    year?
Say thou dost love me, love me, love me – toll
The silver iterance! – only minding, Dear,
To love me also in silence with thy soul.

I lived with visions for my company
Instead of men and women, years ago,
And found them gentle mates, nor thought to know
A sweeter music than they played to me.
But soon their trailing purple was not free
Of this world's dust, – their lutes did silent grow,
And I myself grew faint and blind below
Their vanishing eyes. Then THOU didst come . . . to be,
Belovèd, what they seemed. Their shining fronts,
Their songs, their splendours (better, yet the same,
As river-water hallowed into fonts),
Met in thee, and from out thee overcame
My soul with satisfaction of all wants –
Because God's gifts put man's best dreams to shame.

My letters! all dead paper, . . . mute and white!
And yet they seem alive and quivering
Against my tremulous hands which loose the string
And let them drop down on my knee to-night.
This said, . . . he wished to have me in his sight
Once, as a friend: this fixed a day in spring
To come and touch my hand . . . a simple thing,
Yet I wept for it! – this, . . . the paper's light . . .
Said, *Dear I love thee*; and I sank and quailed
As if God's future thundered on my past.
This said, *I am thine* – and so its ink has paled
With lying at my heart that beat too fast.
And this . . . O Love, thy words have ill availed
If, what this said, I dared repeat at last!

First time he kissed me, he but only kissed
The fingers of this hand wherewith I write;
And ever since, it grew more clean and white,
Slow to world-greetings, quick with its 'Oh, list,'
When the angels speak. A ring of amethyst
I could not wear here, plainer to my sight,
Than that first kiss. The second passed in height
The first, and sought the forehead, and half missed,

Half falling on the hair. O beyond meed!
That was the chrism of love, which love's own
      crown
With sanctifying sweetness, did precede.
The third upon my lips was folded down
In perfect, purple state; since when, indeed,
I have been proud and said, 'My love, my own.'

I thank all who have loved me in their hearts,
With thanks and love from mine. Deep thanks to all
Who paused a little near the prison-wall
To hear my music in its louder parts
Ere they went onward, each one to the mart's
Or temple's occupation, beyond call.
But thou, who, in my voice's sink and fall
When the sob took it, thy divinest Art's
Own instrument didst drop down at thy foot
To harken what I said between my tears, . . .
Instruct me how to thank thee! – Oh, to shoot
My soul's full meaning into future years,
That *they* should lend it utterance, and salute
Love that endures, from Life that disappears!

How do I love thee? Let me count the ways.
I love thee to the depth and breadth and height
My soul can reach, when feeling out of sight
For the ends of Being and ideal Grace.
I love thee to the level of everyday's
Most quiet need, by sun and candlelight.
I love thee freely, as men strive for Right;
I love thee purely, as they turn from Praise.
I love thee with the passion put to use
In my old griefs, and with my childhood's faith.
I love thee with a love I seemed to lose
With my lost saints, – I love thee with the breath,
Smiles, tears, of all my life! – and, if God choose,
I shall but love thee better after death.

Song

Weep, as if you thought of laughter!
Smile, as tears were coming after!
Marry your pleasures to your woes;
And think life's green well worth its rose!

No sorrow will your heart betide,
Without a comfort by its side;
The sun may sleep in his sea-bed,
But you have starlight overhead.

Trust not to Joy! the rose of June,
When opened wide, will wither soon;
Italian days without twilight
Will turn them suddenly to night.

Joy, most changeful of all things,
Flits away on rainbow wings;
And when they look the gayest, know,
It is that they are spread to go!

The Lady's Yes

'Yes,' I answered you last night;
   'No,' this morning, sir, I say.
Colours seen by candle-light
   Will not look the same by day.

When the viols played their best,
   Lamps above and laughs below,
Love me sounded like a jest,
   Fit for *yes* or fit for *no*.

Call me false or call me free,
   Vow, whatever light may shine –
No man on your face shall see
   Any grief for change on mine.

Yet the sin is on us both;
   Time to dance is not to woo;
Wooing light makes fickle troth,
   Scorn of *me* recoils on *you*.

Learn to win a lady's faith
   Nobly, as the thing is high,
Bravely, as for life and death,
   With a loyal gravity.

Lead her from the festive boards,
    Point her to the starry skies;
Guard her, by your truthful words,
    Pure from courtship's flatteries.

By your truth she shall be true,
    Ever true, as wives of yore;
And her *yes*, once said to you,
    SHALL be Yes for evermore.

The Sea-Mew

How joyously the young sea-mew
Lay dreaming on the waters blue
Whereon our little bark had thrown
A little shade, the only one,
But shadows ever man pursue.

Familiar with the waves and free
As if their own white foam were he,
His heart upon the heart of ocean
Lay learning all its mystic motion,
And throbbing to the throbbing sea.

And such a brightness in his eye
As if the ocean and the sky
Within him had lit up and nurst
A soul God gave him not at first,
To comprehend their majesty.

We were not cruel, yet did sunder
His white wing from the blue waves under,
And bound it, while his fearless eyes
Shone up to ours in calm surprise,
As deeming us some ocean wonder.

We bore our ocean bird unto
A grassy place where he might view
The flowers that curtsey to the bees,
The waving of the tall green trees,
The falling of the silver dew.

But flowers of earth were pale to him
Who had seen the rainbow fishes swim;
And when earth's dew around him lay
He thought of ocean's wingèd spray,
And his eye waxed sad and dim.

The green trees round him only made
A prison with their darksome shade;
And drooped his wing, and mournèd he
For his own boundless glittering sea –
Albeit he knew not they could fade.

Then One her gladsome face did bring,
Her gentle voice's murmuring,
In ocean's stead his heart to move
And teach him what was human love:
He thought it a strange mournful thing.

He lay down in his grief to die,
(First looking to the sea-like sky
That hath no waves) because, alas!
Our human touch did on him pass,
And with our touch, our agony.

From
THE CRY OF THE HUMAN

The plague runs festering through the town,
　　And never a bell is tolling,
And corpses, jostled 'neath the moon,
　　Nod to the dead-cart's rolling.
The young child calleth for the cup,
　　The strong man brings it weeping;
The mother from her babe looks up,
　　And shrieks away its sleeping.
　　　　　　　　　　Be pitiful, O God!

The plague of gold strikes far and near,
　　And deep and strong it enters;
This purple chimar which we wear
　　Makes madder than the centaur's:
Our thoughts grow blank, our words grow strange,
　　We cheer the pale gold-diggers –
Each soul is worth so much on 'Change,
　　And marked, like sheep, with figures.
　　　　　　　　　　Be pitiful, O God!

The curse of gold upon the land
　　The lack of bread enforces;
The rail-cars snort from strand to strand,
　　Like more of Death's white horses!

The rich preach 'rights' and 'future days',
   And hear no angel scoffing, –
The poor die mute – with starving gaze
   On corn-ships in the offing.

                    Be pitiful, O God!

We meet together at the feast,
   To private mirth betake us;
We stare down in the winecup, lest
   Some vacant chair should shake us.
We name delight and pledge it round –
   'It shall be ours to-morrow!'
God's seraphs, do your voices sound
   As sad in naming sorrow?

                    Be pitiful, O God!

The happy children come to us,
   And look up in our faces:
They ask us – 'Was it thus, and thus,
   When we were in their places?' –
We cannot speak; – we see anew
   The hills we used to live in,
And feel our mother's smile press through
   The kisses she is giving.

                    Be pitiful, O God!

We sit on hills our childhood wist,
   Woods, hamlets, streams, beholding:
The sun strikes through the farthest mist,
   The city's spire to golden.
The city's golden spire it was,
   When hope and health were strongest,
But now it is the churchyard grass
   We look upon the longest.
                    Be pitiful, O God!

From
THE CRY OF THE CHILDREN

Do ye hear the children weeping, O my brothers,
    Ere the sorrow comes with years?
They are leaning their young heads against their
    mothers,
        And *that* cannot stop their tears.
The young lambs are bleating in the meadows,
    The young birds are chirping in the nest,
The young fawns are playing with the shadows,
    The young flowers are blowing toward the west –
But the young, young children, O my brothers,
        They are weeping bitterly!
They are weeping in the playtime of the others,
        In the country of the free.

Do you question the young children in the sorrow
        Why their tears are falling so?
The old man may weep for his to-morrow
        Which is lost in Long Ago;
The old tree is leafless in the forest,
    The old year is ending in the frost,
The old wound, if stricken, is the sorest,
    The old hope is hardest to be lost.
But the young, young children, O my brothers,
        Do you ask them why they stand
Weeping sore before the bosoms of their mothers,
        In our happy Fatherland?

'For oh,' say the children, 'we are weary,
　　　And we cannot run or leap;
If we cared for any meadows, it were merely
　　　To drop down in them and sleep.
Our knees tremble sorely in the stooping,
　　We fall upon our faces, trying to go;
And, underneath our heavy eyelids drooping,
　　The reddest flower would look as pale as snow;
For, all day, we drag our burden tiring
　　　Through the coal-dark, underground –
Or, all day, we drive the wheels of iron
　　　In the factories, round and round.'

They look up with their pale and sunken faces,
　　　And their look is dread to see,
For they mind you of their angels in high places,
　　　With eyes turned on Deity! –
'How long,' they say, 'how long, O cruel nation,
　　Will you stand, to move the world, on a child's
　　　　heart, –
Stifle down with a mailed heel its palpitation,
　　And tread onward to your throne amid the mart?
Our blood splashes upward, O gold-heaper,
　　　And your purple shows your path!
But the child's sob in the silence curses deeper
　　　Than the strong man in his wrath.'

That Day

I stand by the river where both of us stood,
And there is but one shadow to darken the flood;
And the path leading to it, where both used to pass,
Has the step but of one, to take dew from the grass, –
   One forlorn since that day.

The flowers of the margin are many to see;
None stoops at my bidding to pluck them for me.
The bird in the alder sings loudly and long, –
My low sound of weeping disturbs not his song,
   As thy vow did, that day.

I stand by the river, I think of the vow;
Oh, calm as the place is, vow-breaker, be thou!
I leave the flower growing, the bird unreproved;
Would I trouble *thee* rather than *them*, my belovèd, –
   And my lover that day?

Go, be sure of my love, by that treason forgiven;
Of my prayers, by the blessings they win thee from
   Heaven;
Of my grief – (guess the length of the sword by the
   sheath's)
By the silence of life, more pathetic than death's!
   Go, – be clear of that day!

Flush or Faunus

You see this dog. It was but yesterday
I mused forgetful of his presence here
Till thought on thought drew downward tear on
    tear,
When from the pillow where wet-cheeked I lay,
A head as hairy as Faunus thrust its way
Right sudden against my face, – two golden-clear
Great eyes astonished mine, – a drooping ear
Did flap me on either cheek to dry the spray!
I started first as some Arcadian
Amazed by goatly god in twilight grove,
But as the bearded vision closelier ran
My tears off, I knew Flush, and rose above
Surprise and sadness, – thanking the true PAN
Who, by low creatures, leads to heights of love.

From
A SABBATH MORNING
AT SEA

The ship went on with solemn face;
　　To meet the darkness on the deep,
　　　　The solemn ship went onward.
I bowed down weary in the place,
　　For parting tears and present sleep
　　　　Had weighed mine eyelids downward.

The new sight, the new wondrous sight!
　　The waters round me, turbulent, –
　　　　The skies impassive o'er me,
Calm, in a moonless, sunless light,
　　Half glorified by that intent
　　　　Of holding the day-glory!

Love me, sweet friends, this sabbath day!
　　The sea sings round me while ye roll
　　　　Afar the hymn unaltered,
And kneel, where once I knelt to pray,
　　And bless me deeper in the soul,
　　　　Because the voice has faltered.

And though this sabbath comes to me
    Without the stolèd minister
        Or chanting congregation,
God's spirit brings communion, HE
    Who brooded soft on waters drear,
        Creator on creation.

Himself, I think, shall draw me higher,
    Where keep the saints with harp and song
        An endless sabbath morning,
And on that sea commixed with fire
    Oft drop their eyelids, raised too long
        To the full Godhead's burning.

Hiram Powers' 'Greek Slave'

They say Ideal beauty cannot enter
The house of anguish. On the threshold stands
An alien Image with enshackled hands,
Called the Greek Slave! as if the artist meant her
(That passionless perfection which he lent her,
Shadowed not darkened where the sill expands)
To so confront man's crimes in different lands
With man's ideal sense. Pierce to the centre,
Art's fiery finger! – and break up ere long
The serfdom of this world! Appeal, fair stone,
From God's pure heights of beauty against man's
        wrong!
Catch up in thy divine face, not alone
East griefs but west, – and strike and shame the
        strong,
By thunders of white silence, overthrown.

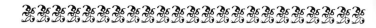

Life

Each creature holds an insular point in space;
Yet what man stirs a finger, breathes a sound,
But all the multitudinous beings round
In all the countless worlds with time and place
For their conditions, down to the central base,
Thrill, haply, in vibration and rebound,
Life answering life across the vast profound,
In full antiphony, by a common grace?
I think this sudden joyaunce which illumes
A child's mouth sleeping, unaware may run
From some soul newly loosened from earth's tombs:
I think this passionate sigh, which half-begun
I stifle back, may reach and stir the plumes
Of God's calm angel standing in the sun.

Question and Answer

Love you seek for, presupposes
  Summer heat and sunny glow.
Tell me, do you find moss-roses
  Budding, blooming in the snow?
Snow might kill the rose-tree's root —
Shake it quickly from your foot,
  Lest it harm you as you go.

From the ivy where it dapples
  A grey ruin, stone by stone, —
Do you look for grapes and apples,
  Or for sad green leaves alone?
Pluck the leaves off, two or three —
Keep them for morality
  When you shall be safe and gone.

From
CROWNED AND BURIED

NAPOLEON! – years ago, and that great word
Compact of human breath in hate and dread
And exultation, skied us overhead –
An atmosphere whose lightning was the sword
Scathing the cedars of the world, – drawn down
In burnings, by the metal of a crown.

That name consumed the silence of the snows
In Alpine keeping, holy and cloud-hid;
The mimic eagles dared what Nature's did,
And over-rushed her moutainous repose
In search of eyries: and the Egyptian river
Mingled the same word with its grand 'For ever.'

That name was shouted near the pyramidal
Nilotic tombs, whose mummied habitants,
Packed to humanity's significance,
Motioned it back with stillness, – shouts as idle
As hireling artists' work of myrrh and spice
Which swathed last glories around the Ptolemies.

The world's face changed to hear it: kingly men
Came down in chidden babes' bewilderment
From autocratic places, each content
With sprinkled ashes for anointing: then
The people laughed or wondered for the nonce,
To see one throne a composite of thrones.

Napoleon! – 'twas a high name lifted high:
It met at last God's thunder sent to clear
Our compassing and covering atmosphere
And open a clear sight beyond the sky
Of supreme empire; this of earth's was done –
And kings crept out again to feel the sun.

From
DE PROFUNDIS

The face which, duly as the sun,
Rose up for me with life begun,
To mark all bright hours of the day
With hourly love, is dimmed away, –
And yet my days go on, go on.

The tongue which, like a stream, could run
Smooth music from the roughest stone,
And every morning with 'Good day'
Make each day good, is hushed away, –
And yet my days go on, go on.

The heart which, like a staff, was one
For mine to lean and rest upon,
The strongest on the longest day
With steadfast love, is caught away, –
And yet my days go on, go on.

The past rolls forward on the sun
And makes all night. O dreams begun,
Not to be ended! Ended bliss,
And life that will not end in this!
My days go on, my days go on.

I knock and cry, – Undone, undone!
Is there no help, no comfort, – none?
No gleaning in the wide wheat-plains
Where others drive their loaded wains?
My vacant days go on, go on.

Only to lift the turf unmown
From off the earth where it has grown,
Some cubit-space, and say 'Behold,
Creep in, poor Heart, beneath that fold,
Forgetting how the days go on.'

Take from my head the thorn-wreath brown!
No mortal grief deserves that crown.
O supreme Love, chief misery,
The sharp regalia are for THEE
Whose days eternally go on!

And having in thy life-depth thrown
Being and suffering (which are one),
As a child drops his pebble small
Down some deep well, and hears it fall
Smiling – so I. THY DAYS GO ON.

From
CASA GUIDI WINDOWS

Cimabue stood up very well
In spite of Giotto's, and Angelico
   The artist-saint kept smiling in his cell
The smile with which he welcomed the sweet slow
   Inbreak of angels (whitening through the dim
That he might paint them), while the sudden sense
   Of Raffael's future was revealed to him
By force of his own fair works' competence.
   The same blue waters where the dolphins swim
Suggest the tritons. Through the blue Immense
   Strike out, all swimmers! cling not in the way
Of one another, so to sink; but learn
   The strong man's impulse, catch the freshening
      spray
He throws up in his motions, and discern
   By his clear westering eye, the time of day.

Cold graves, we say? it shall be testified
That living men who burn in heart and brain,
  Without the dead were colder. If we tried
To sink the past beneath our feet, be sure
  The future would not stand. Precipitate
This old roof from the shrine, and, insecure,
  The nesting swallows fly off, mate from mate.
How scant the gardens, if the graves were fewer!
  The tall green poplars grew no longer straight
Whose tops not looked to Troy. Would any fight
  For Athens, and not swear by Marathon?
Who dared build temples, without tombs in sight?
  Or live, without some dead man's benison?
Or seek truth, hope for good, and strive for right,
  If, looking up, he saw not in the sun
Some angel of the martyrs all day long
  Standing and waiting? Your last rhythm will need
Your earliest key-note. Could I sing this song,
  If my dead masters had not taken heed
To help the heavens and earth to make me strong,
  As the wind ever will find out some reed
And touch it to such issues as belong
  To such a frail thing? None may grudge the Dead
Libations from full cups. Unless we choose
  To look back to the hills behind us spread,
The plains before us sadden and confuse;
  If orphaned, we are disinherited.

From
BIANCA AMONG THE NIGHTINGALES

The cypress stood up like a church
  That night we felt our love would hold,
And saintly moonlight seemed to search
  And wash the whole world clean as gold;
The olives crystallized the vales'
  Broad slopes until the hills grew strong:
The fireflies and the nightingales
  Throbbed each to either, flame and song.
The nightingales, the nightingales!

Upon the angle of its shade
  The cypress stood, self-balanced high;
Half up, half down, as double made,
  Along the ground, against the sky.
And *we* too! from such soul-height went
  Such leaps of blood, so blindly driven,
We scarce knew if our nature meant
  Most passionate earth or intense heaven.
The nightingales, the nightingales!

Giulio, my Giulio! – sing they so,
    And you be silent? Do I speak,
And you not hear? An arm you throw
    Round some one, and I feel so weak?
– Oh, owl-like birds! They sing for spite,
    They sing for hate, they sing for doom!
They'll sing through death who sing through night,
    They'll sing and stun me in the tomb –
The nightingales, the nightingales!

From
AURORA LEIGH

Aurora's Independence

With quiet indignation I broke in,
'You misconceive the question like a man,
Who sees a woman as the complement
Of his sex merely. You forget too much
That every creature, female as the male,
Stands single in responsible act and thought
As also in birth and death. Whoever says
To a loyal woman, "Love and work with me,"
Will get fair answers if the work and love,
Being good themselves, are good for her – the best
She was born for. Women of a softer mood,
Surprised by men when scarcely awake to life,
Will sometimes only hear the first word, love,
And catch up with it any kind of work,
Indifferent, so that dear love go with it.
I do not blame such women, though, for love,
They pick much oakum; earth's fanatics make
Too frequently heaven's saints. But *me* your work
Is not the best for, – nor your love the best,
Nor able to commend the kind of work
For love's sake merely.'

A Prospect of Florence

I found a house at Florence on the hill
Of Bellosguardo. 'Tis a tower which keeps
A post of double observation o'er
That valley of Arno (holding as a hand
The outspread city) straight towards Fiesole
And Mount Morello and the setting sun,
The Vallombrosan mountains opposite,
Which sunrise fills as full as crystal cups
Turned red to the brim because their wine is red.
No sun could die nor yet be born unseen
By dwellers at my villa: morn and eve
Were magnified before us in the pure
Illimitable space and pause of sky,
Intense as angels' garments blanched with God,
Less blue than radiant. From the outer wall
Of the garden, drops the mystic floating grey
Of olive trees (with interruptions green
From maise and vine), until 'tis caught and torn
Upon the abrupt black line of cypresses
Which signs the way to Florence. Beautiful
The city lies along the ample vale,
Cathedral, tower and palace, piazza and street,
The river trailing like a silver cord
Through all, and curling loosely, both before
And after, over the whole stretch of land
Sown whitely up and down its opposite slopes
With farms and villas.

SOURCES OF THE EXTRACTS

Suite of Sonnets
This selection of sonnets from the complete set, *Sonnets from the Portuguese*, has been chosen to tell the story, or, more accurately, to chart the relationship, of the poet and her lover (Elizabeth to Robert), while printing only the most attractive and accomplished works of the full complement of forty-four. The sonnets included are numbered 3, 4, 5, 10, 13, 14, 21, 26, 28, 38, 41 and 43 in the original sequence.

The Cry of the Human
Abridged from the original; stanzas 4, 5, 6, 7, 10 and 13 only are included.

The Cry of the Children
Shortened: stanzas 1, 2, 6 and 13 only are printed.

A Sabbath Morning at Sea
Shortened to include only the stanzas set by Elgar in his *Sea Pictures* – numbers 1, 3, 11, 12 and 13 of the original.

Crowned and Buried
Another long poem abridged to its essence to concentrate on the portrait of Napoleon and on his influence on dynastic Europe. Consists of stanzas 1, 4, 5, 6 and 11.

De Profundis
Stanzas 1, 2, 3, 6, 8, 12, 20 and 24 only are reproduced.

Bianca Among the Nightingales
Drastically revised to turn a discursive love poem into a lyric – stanzas 1, 2 and 16 only.

Casa Guidi Windows
First extract: Book One, lines 389–403; second extract: Book One, lines 415–41.

Aurora Leigh
First extract: Book Two, lines 434–53; second extract: Book Seven, lines 515–41.

NOTES ON THE PICTURES

EMILY DICKINSON

Emily
Dickinson

INTRODUCTION

Emily Dickinson was born in Amherst, Massachusetts, in 1830 and died there in 1886. The family was a distinguished one: Emily's grandfather had founded Amherst College, and her father was a lawyer and State Congressman. Emily herself was renowned for her wit in a lively and sociable household – until her middle twenties. From that time on she became a recluse.

Speculation has it that the reason was unrequited love. Emily's niece, Martha Dickinson (Bianchi), said that she 'met her fate' in the person of a renowned Philadelphia preacher. This can only have been the Reverend Charles Wadsworth, with whom we know for certain she cultivated an 'intellectual friendship'. Other names, and reasons, have been advanced for Emily's self-imposed retirement.

What is important to us, however, is her poetry. This did not come to light until after her death, when her sister Lavinia handed over some of Emily's papers to 'Sister Sue', her brother's wife. Sue entrusted the work of editing to Professor and Mrs Todd of Amherst College. From the approximately 700 poems then discovered, Mrs Todd (with the help of Thomas Wentworth Higginson) brought out the *First Series* of Emily's poems in 1890. Two more *Series* appeared, in 1891 and 1896, all considerably doctored by the correct and somewhat embarrassed Higginson. More poems, under the title of *The Single Hound*, came out in 1914, edited by Martha Dickinson Bianchi. *Further Poems* by Mrs Bianchi and Alfred Leete Hampson was published in 1929, and the first collected volume, *The Poems of Emily Dickinson*, by the same editors, appeared in 1937.

It was known for many years that this text, like the Todd–Higginson ones, was by no means accurate; but friends and relatives kept the manuscripts jealously guarded until the 1950s, when Thomas H. Johnson of the Lawrenceville School, New Jersey, was allowed to see all the manuscripts. In 1955 he published his three-volume variorum edition of *The Poems of Emily Dickinson* and it was revealed that the actual number of Emily's poems stood at 1775. In 1960 Mr Johnson made a one-volume edition, and it is from this that the present selection was made.*

On 15 April 1862, when Emily was thirty-one years old, she had written to Higginson, a well-known New England 'man of letters', enclosing four of her poems. She wished to know whether her verses 'breathed'. We do not have his reply but we have Emily's side of the correspondence. 'You think,' she says, 'my gait "spasmodic". I am in no danger, Sir. You think me "uncontrolled". I have no Tribunal . . . The Sailor cannot see the North, but knows the Needle can.'

So much for Higginson – put firmly in his place. Emily Dickinson knew herself a true poet and she did not need contemporary endorsement. Indeed, the poems of the sixties are much concerned with 'fame', as if she were anticipating what was to come after her death. Like most good poets, she expressed herself

Publisher's note. It is regretted that, for copyright reasons, the Harvard variorum edition from which Geoffrey Moore made his selection could not be used, and it is the earlier versions of the poems which are printed here. The discrepancies between what Emily Dickinson wrote and the 'improvements' made by her nineteenth-century editors are listed on p. 59.

more frequently through metaphor than simile, and her metaphors first make the reader pause at their strangeness – and then agree to their justness. Contemporary as she was with the late-Romantic Victorians, she could not avoid a certain amount of whimsicality; but this is very small. 'I like to see it lap the miles': on the face of it an ecstatic young lady's cry, yields, at a closer look, an odd and typical ambiguity. Her metaphors, 'gazing grain', 'zero at the bone', are as penetrating as her irony ('Because I could not stop for Death, He kindly stopped for me'), which reaches the point of paradox in 'Parting is all we know of heaven/ And all we need of hell.'

Her persistent use of Common Metre and the hymn-like, nursery rhyme-like regularity of her stanza must be set against the grimness of her images, her dramatic shifts of tone and the truly metaphysical cast of her imagination. Emily Dickinson had the power and perception of a great poet. Unfortunately her professional skill did not match her poetic vision – a fact of which she may well have been aware. Unwilling, therefore, to subvert this vision to her comparatively poor craft, we might speculate that she 'let herself go'. The result is the extraordinary combination of unorthodoxy and accuracy which we find in Emily's poems: a unique combination of prosodic idiosyncracy and moral insight. Through the power of her imagination she transformed her personal experience into universal truth. After Whitman – so different in style yet so similar in his independence – Emily Dickinson is the most important American poet of the nineteenth century.

GEOFFREY MOORE

Exultation is the going
Of an inland soul to sea, –
Past the houses, past the headlands,
Into deep eternity!

Bred as we, among the mountains,
Can the sailor understand
The divine intoxication
Of the first league out from land?

❧❧❧

I never hear the word 'escape'
Without a quicker blood,
A sudden expectation,
A flying attitude.

I never hear of prisons broad
By soldiers battered down,
But I tug childish at my bars, –
Only to fail again!

Success is counted sweetest
By those who ne'er succeed.
To comprehend a nectar
Requires sorest need.

Not one of all the purple Host
Who took the flag to-day
Can tell the definition,
So clear, of victory,

As he, defeated, dying,
On whose forbidden ear
The distant strains of triumph
Break agonized and clear.

Some things that fly there be,—
Birds, hours, the bumble-bee:
Of these no elegy.

Some things that stay there be,—
Grief, hills, eternity:
Nor this behooveth me.

There are, that resting, rise.
Can I expound the skies?
How still the riddle lies!

To fight aloud is very brave,
But gallanter, I know,
Who charge within the bosom,
The cavalry of woe.

Who win, and nations do not see,
Who fall, and none observe,
Whose dying eyes no country
Regards with patriot love.

We trust, in plumed procession,
For such the angels go,
Rank after rank, with even feet
And uniforms of snow.

An altered look about the hills;
A Tyrian light the village fills;
A wider sunrise in the dawn;
A deeper twilight on the lawn;
A print of a vermillion foot;
A purple finger on the slope;
A flippant fly upon the pane;
A spider at his trade again;
An added strut in chanticleer;
A flower expected everywhere;
An axe shrill singing in the woods;
Fern-odors on untravelled roads,
All this, and more I cannot tell,
A furtive look you know as well,
And Nicodemus' mystery
Receives its annual reply.

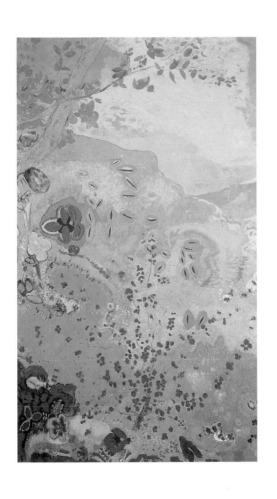

I taste a liquor never brewed,
From tankards scooped in pearl;
Not all the vats upon the Rhine
Yield such an alcohol!

Inebriate of air am I,
And debauchee of dew,
Reeling, through endless summer days,
From inns of molten blue.

When landlords turn the drunken bee
Out of the foxglove's door,
When butterflies renounce their drams,
I shall but drink the more!

Till seraphs swing their snowy hats,
And saints to windows run,
To see the little tippler
Leaning against the sun!

Safe in their alabaster chambers,
Untouched by morning and untouched by noon,
Sleep the meek members of the resurrection,
Rafter of satin, and roof of stone.

Light laughs the breeze in her castle of sunshine,
Babbles the bee in a stolid ear;
Pipe the sweet birds in ignorant cadence,
Ah, what sagacity perished here!

Grand go the years in the crescent above them;
Worlds scoop their arcs, and firmaments row,
Diadems drop and Doges surrender,
Soundless as dots on a disk of snow.

Hope is the thing with feathers
That perches in the soul,
And sings the tune without the words,
And never stops at all,

And sweetest in the gale is heard;
And sore must be the storm
That could abash the little bird
That kept so many warm.

I've heard it in the chillest land,
And on the strangest sea;
Yet, never, in extremity,
It asked a crumb of me.

I like a look of agony,
Because I know it's true;
Men do not sham convulsion,
Nor simulate a throe.

The eyes glaze once, and that is death.
Impossible to feign
The beads upon the forehead
By homely anguish strung.

❧❧❧

I'm nobody! Who are you?
Are you nobody, too?
Then there's a pair of us—don't tell!
They'd banish us, you know.

How dreary to be somebody!
How public, like a frog
To tell your name the livelong day
To an admiring bog!

I felt a funeral in my brain,
And mourners, to and fro,
Kept treading, treading, till it seemed
That sense was breaking through.

And when they all were seated,
A service like a drum
Kept beating, beating, till I thought
My mind was going numb.

And then I heard them lift a box,
And creak across my soul
With those same boots of lead, again.
Then space began to toll

As all the heavens were a bell,
And being but an ear,
And I and silence some strange race,
Wrecked, solitary, here.

There's a certain slant of light,
On winter afternoons,
That oppresses, like the weight
Of cathedral tunes.

Heavenly hurt it gives us;
We can find no scar,
But internal difference,
Where the meanings are.

None may teach it anything,
'T is the seal, despair, –
An imperial affliction
Sent us of the air.

When it comes, the landscape listens,
Shadows hold their breath;
When it goes, 't is like the distance
On the look of death.

The soul selects her own society,
Then shuts the door;
On her divine majority
Obtrude no more.

Unmoved, she notes the chariot's pausing
At her low gate;
Unmoved, an emperor be kneeling
Upon her mat.

I've known her from an ample nation
Choose one;
Then close the valves of her attention
Like stone.

Some keep the Sabbath going to church;
I keep it staying at home,
With a bobolink for a chorister,
And an orchard for a dome.

Some keep the Sabbath in surplice,
I just wear my wings,
And instead of tolling the bell for church
Our little sexton sings.

God preaches,—a noted clergyman,—
And the sermon is never long;
So instead of getting to heaven at last,
I'm going all along!

I'll tell you how the sun rose,
A ribbon at a time.
The steeples swam in amethyst,
The news like squirrels ran.

The hills untied their bonnets,
The bobolinks begun.
Then I said softly to myself,
'That must have been the sun!'

.   .   .   .

But how he set, I know not.
There seemed a purple stile
That little yellow boys and girls
Were climbing all the while

Till when they reached the other side,
A dominie in gray
Put gently up the evening bars,
And led the flock away.

What soft, cherubic creatures
These gentlewomen are!
One would as soon assault a plush
Or violate a star.

Such dimity convictions,
A horror so refined
Of freckled human nature,
Of Deity ashamed,

It's such a common glory,
A fisherman's degree!
Redemption, brittle lady,
Be so, ashamed of thee.

I heard a fly buzz when I died;
The stillness round my form
Was like the stillness in the air
Between the heaves of storm.

The eyes beside had wrung them dry,
And breaths were gathering sure
For that last onset, when the king
Be witnessed in his power.

I willed my keepsakes, signed away
What portion of me I
Could make assignable, and then
There interposed a fly,

With blue, uncertain stumbling buzz,
Between the light and me;
And then the windows failed, and then
I could not see to see.

A bird came down the walk;
He did not know I saw;
He bit an angle-worm in halves
And ate the fellow, raw.

And then he drank a dew
From a convenient grass,
And then hopped sidewise to the wall
To let a beetle pass.

He glanced with rapid eyes
That hurried all abroad,—
They looked like frightened beads, I thought;
He stirred his velvet head

Like one in danger; cautious,
I offered him a crumb,
And he unrolled his feathers
And rowed him softer home

Than oars divide the ocean,
Too silver for a seam,
Or butterflies, off banks of noon,
Leap, plashless, as they swim.

I died for beauty, but was scarce
Adjusted in the tomb,
When one who died for truth was lain
In an adjoining room.

He questioned softly why I failed?
'For beauty,' I replied.
'And I for truth,–the two are one;
We brethren, are,' he said.

And so, as kinsmen, met a night,
We talked between the rooms,
Until the moss had reached our lips,
And covered up our names.

Much madness is divinest sense
To a discerning eye;
Much sense the starkest madness.
'T is the majority
In this, as all, prevails.
Assent, and you are sane;
Demur, you're straightway dangerous,
And handled with a chain.

The heart asks pleasure first,
And then, excuse from pain;
And then, those little anodynes
That deaden suffering;

And then, to go to sleep;
And then, if it should be
The will of its Inquisitor,
The liberty to die.

It was not death, for I stood up,
And all the dead lie down;
It was not night, for all the bells
Put out their tongues, for noon.

It was not frost, for on my flesh
I felt siroccos crawl,
Nor fire, for just my marble feet
Could keep a chancel cool.

And yet it tasted like them all;
The figures I have seen
Set orderly, for burial,
Reminded me of mine,

As if my life were shaven
And fitted to a frame,
And could not breathe without a key;
And 't was like midnight, some,

When everything that ticked has stopped,
And space stares, all around,
Or grisly frosts, first autumn morns,
Repeal the beating ground.

But most like chaos,—stopless, cool,—
Without a chance or spar,
Or even a report of land
To justify despair.

If you were coming in the fall,
I'd brush the summer by
With half a smile and half a spurn,
As housewives do a fly.

If I could see you in a year,
I'd wind the months in balls,
And put them each in separate drawers,
Until their time befalls.

If only centuries delayed,
I'd count them on my hand,
Subtracting till my fingers dropped
Into Van Diemen's land.

If certain, when this life was out,
That yours and mine, should be,
I'd toss it yonder, like a rind,
And taste eternity.

But now, uncertain of the length
Of time's uncertain wing,
It goads me, like the goblin bee,
That will not state its sting.

I like to see it lap the miles,
And lick the valleys up,
And stop to feed itself at tanks;
And then, prodigious, step

Around a pile of mountains,
And, supercilious, peer
In shanties by the sides of roads;
And then a quarry pare

To fit its sides, and crawl between,
Complaining all the while
In horrid hooting stanza;
Then chase itself down hill

And neigh like Boanerges;
Then, punctual as a star,
Stop—docile and omnipotent—
At its own stable door.

It makes no difference abroad,
The seasons fit the same,
The mornings blossom into noons,
And split their pods of flame.

Wild-flowers kindle in the woods,
The brooks brag all the day;
No blackbird bates his jargoning
For passing Calvary.

Auto-da-fé and judgment
Are nothing to the bee;
His separation from his rose
To him seems misery.

The brain is wider than the sky,
For, put them side by side,
The one the other will include
With ease, and you beside.

The brain is deeper than the sea,
For, hold them, blue to blue,
The one the other will absorb,
As sponges, buckets do.

The brain is just the weight of God,
For, lift them, pound for pound,
And they will differ, if they do,
As syllable from sound.

I've seen a dying eye
Run round and round a room
In search of something, as it seemed,
Then cloudier become;
And then, obscure with fog,
And then, be soldered down,
Without disclosing what it be,
'T were blessed to have seen.

❦❦❦

I asked no other thing,
No other was denied.
I offered Being for it;
The mighty merchant smiled.

Brazil? He twirled a button,
Without a glance my way:
'But, madam, is there nothing else
That we can show to-day?'

Because I could not stop for Death,
He kindly stopped for me;
The carriage held but just ourselves
And Immortality.

We slowly drove, he knew no haste,
And I had put away
My labor, and my leisure too,
For his civility.

We passed the school where children played,
Their lessons scarcely done;
We passed the fields of gazing grain,
We passed the setting sun.

We paused before a house that seemed
A swelling of the ground;
The roof was scarcely visible,
The cornice but a mound.

Since then 't is centuries; but each
Feels shorter than the day
I first surmised the horses' heads
Were toward eternity.

I cannot live with you,
It would be life,
And life is over there
Behind the shelf

The sexton keeps the key to,
Putting up
Our life, his porcelain,
Like a cup

Discarded of the housewife,
Quaint or broken;
A newer Sèvres pleases,
Old ones crack.

I could not die with you,
For one must wait
To shut the other's gaze down,
You could not.

And I, could I stand by
And see you freeze,
Without my right of frost,
Death's privilege?

Nor could I rise with you,
Because your face
Would put out Jesus',
That new grace

Glow plain and foreign
On my homesick eye,

Except that you, than he
Shone closer by.

They'd judge us—how?
For you served heaven, you know,
Or sought to,
I could not,

Because you saturated sight,
And I had no more eyes
For sordid excellence
As Paradise.

And were you lost, I would be,
Though my name
Rang loudest
On the heavenly fame.

And were you saved,
And I condemned to be
Where you were not,
That self were hell to me.

So we must meet apart,
You there, I here,
With just the door ajar
That oceans are,
And prayer,
And that pale sustenance,
Despair!

A narrow fellow in the grass
Occasionally rides;
You may have met him,—did you not,
His notice sudden is.

The grass divides as with a comb,
A spotted shaft is seen;
And then it closes at your feet
And opens further on.

He likes a boggy acre,
A floor too cool for corn.
Yet when a child, and barefoot,
I more than once, at morn,

Have passed, I thought, a whip-lash
Unbraiding in the sun,—
When, stooping to secure it,
It wrinkled, and was gone.

Several of nature's people
I know and they know me;
I feel for them a transport
Of cordiality;

But never met this fellow,
Attended or alone,
Without a tighter breathing,
And zero at the bone.

I years had been from home,
And now, before the door,
I dared not open, lest a face
I never saw before

Stare vacant into mine
And ask my business there.
My business,—just a life I left,
Was such still dwelling there?

I fumbled at my nerve,
I scanned the windows near;
The silence like an ocean rolled,
And broke against my ear.

I laughed a wooden laugh
That I could fear a door,
Who danger and the dead had faced,
And never quaked before.

I fitted to the latch
My hand, with trembling care,
Lest back the awful door should spring,
And leave me standing there.

I moved my fingers off
As cautiously as glass,
And held my ears, and like a thief
Fled gasping from the house.

Ample make this bed.
Make this bed with awe;
In it wait till judgment break
Excellent and fair.

Be its mattress straight,
Be its pillow round;
Let no sunrise' yellow noise
Interrupt this ground.

I felt a clearing in my mind
As if my brain had split;
I tried to match it, seam by seam,
But could not make them fit.

The thought behind I strove to join
Unto the thought before,
But sequence ravelled out of reach
Like balls upon a floor.

There came a wind like a bugle;
It quivered through the grass,
And a green chill upon the heat
So ominous did pass
We barred the windows and the doors
As from an emerald ghost;
The doom's electric moccasin
That very instant passed.
On a strange mob of panting trees,
And fences fled away,
And rivers where the houses ran
The living looked that day.
The bell within the steeple wild
The flying tidings whirled.
How much can come
And much can go,
And yet abide the world!

I never saw a moor;
I never saw the sea;
Yet know I how the heather looks,
And what a wave must be.

I never spoke with God,
Nor visited in heaven;
Yet certain am I of the spot
As if the chart were given.

❧❧❧

At half-past three a single bird
Unto a silent sky
Propounded but a single term
Of cautious melody.

At half-past four, experiment
Had subjugated test,
And lo! her silver principle
Supplanted all the rest.

At half-past seven, element
Nor implement was seen.
And place was where the presence was,
Circumference between.

The last night that she lived,
It was a common night,
Except the dying; this to us
Made nature different.

We noticed smallest things,—
Things overlooked before,
By this great light upon our minds
Italicized, as 't were.

That others could exist
While she must finish quite,
A jealousy for her arose
So nearly infinite.

We waited while she passed;
It was a narrow time,
Too jostled were our souls to speak,
At length the notice came.

She mentioned, and forgot;
Then lightly as a reed
Bent to the water, shivered scarce,
Consented, and was dead.

And we, we placed the hair,
And drew the head erect;
And then an awful leisure was,
Our faith to regulate.

We never know how high we are
Till we are called to rise;
And then, if we are true to plan,
Our statures touch the skies.

The heroism we recite
Would be a daily thing,
Did not ourselves the cubits warp
For fear to be a king.

❦❦❦

My life closed twice before its close;
It yet remains to see
If Immortality unveil
A third event to me

So huge, so hopeless to conceive
As these that twice befell.
Parting is all we know of heaven,
And all we need of hell.

NOTES ON THE POEMS

Where there are differences between the actual words used by Emily Dickinson in the poems published in the Harvard variorum edition and those printed in this book, these are listed below. Discrepancies in punctuation and spelling are not noted.

p.79 1.5: Light laughs the breeze/In her Castle above them–

p.82 'I'm nobody! Who are you?' 1.4: Don't tell! they'd advertise–you know! 1.7: To tell one's name–the livelong June–

p.83 A fifth verse: And then a Plank in Reason, broke,/And I dropped down, and down–/And hit a World at every plunge,/And finished knowing–then–

p.84 1.3: That oppresses, like the Heft 1.9: None may teach it–Any–/'Tis the Seal Despair

p.86 1.3: On her divine Majority–/Present no more–

p.91 1.2: The Stillness in the Room 1.5: The Eyes around–had wrung them dry–/And Breaths were gathering firm 1.8: Be witnessed–in the Room– 1.10: What portion of me be/Assignable–and then it was

p.93 1.10: That hurried all around

p.94 1.7: 'And I–for Truth–Themself are One–

p.95 'The heart asks pleasure first' 1.8: The privilege to die–

p.98 1.8: For fear the numbers fuse– 1.16: And take Eternity– 1.18: Of this, that is between,

p.99 1.9: To fit its Ribs/And Crawl between

p.100 1.6: The Brooks slam–all the Day–/No Black bird bates his Banjo– 1.12: To Him–sums Misery–

p.102 1.3: The one the other will contain 1.10: For–Heft them–Pound for Pound–

p.103 'I asked no other thing' 1.4: The Mighty Merchant sneered–

p.105 1.9: We passed the School, where Children strove/At Recess in the Ring–/ A fourth verse: Or rather–He passed Us–/The Dews drew quivering and chill–/For only Gossamer, my Gown–/My Tippet–only Tulle– 1.16: The Cornice–in the Ground–/Since then–'tis Centuries–and yet

p.107 1.24: And that White Sustenance–

p.108 1.11: Yet when a Boy, and Barefoot–/I more than once at Noon

p.110 1.3: I dared not enter, lest a Face 1.5: Stare stolid into mine 1.7: My Business but a Life I left/Was such remaining there?'/I leaned upon the Awe–/I lingered with Before–/The Second like an Ocean rolled/And broke against my ear–/I laughed a crumbling Laugh/That I could fear a Door/Who Consternation compassed/And never winced before. 1.20: And leave me in the Floor–/Then moved my Fingers off

NOTES ON THE PICTURES

p.66 Mary Newcomb (b. 1922). *A Hedge in November*, 1984. Oil on canvas.
Private collection. Reproduced by permission of the artist. Photo:
Crane Kalman Gallery, London.

p.73 Winifred Nicholson (1893–1981). *Rocky Coast, Rough Sea*, 1971. Oil
on canvas. Private collection. Photo: Crane Kalman Gallery, London.

p.77 Odilon Redon (1840–1916). *Day* (left-hand leaf), 1910–11. Distemper
on wood. Fontfroide Abbey, Aude. Photo: Gruppo Editoriale Fabbri,
Milan.

p.80 Winifred Nicholson. *The Gate to the Isles*, 1981. Oil on canvas. Private
collection. Photo: Crane Kalman Gallery, London.

p.85 John Nash (1893–1977). *Wintry Evening, a Pond*, 1958. Watercolour.
Private collection. Reproduced by permission of the Artistic Trustee
of the John Nash Estate.

p.89 Winifred Nicholson. *Daybreak*, 1970. Oil on canvas. Private collec-
tion. Photo: Crane Kalman Gallery, London.

p.92 Mary Newcomb. *Bullfinch inside a Bush*, 1984. Oil on canvas. Repro-
duced by permission of the artist. Photo: Crane Kalman Gallery,
London.

p.97 Albert Pinkham Ryder (1847–1917). *Toilers of the Sea*, before 1844.
Oil on wood. Metropolitan Museum of Art, New York. George A.
Hearn Fund, 1915.

p.101 Mary Newcomb. *Bees in Lavender*, 1984. Oil on canvas. Private collec-
tion. Reproduced by permission of the artist. Photo: Crane Kalman
Gallery, London.

p.104 André Derain (1880–1954). *Effets de soleil sur l'eau*, 1905. Oil on
canvas. Musée de l'Annonciade, St Tropez. Photo: Réunion des
Musées Nationaux. © ADAGP, 1986.

CHRISTINA ROSSETTI

Christina
Rossetti

INTRODUCTION

Before 1900 the list of women authors in English is short, and of poets, much shorter. Aphra Behn wrote plays and Jane Austen and George Eliot were pre-eminent as novelists. Apart from little known eighteenth-century names, such as those of Mary Leapor and Anna Seward, the feminine authorial roll-call amounts to just Elizabeth Barrett Browning, the Brontë sisters and Christina Rossetti. All were Victorians and, in their several ways, eminently Victorian. The greatest, undoubtedly, was Christina Rossetti, which makes her the finest woman poet in English literature. (Not, of course, in English-language literature. America has Emily Dickinson, and she is one of the supreme poets of all ages and languages.)

It does Christina Rossetti little justice to categorize her as a 'woman poet'. She is a very original writer, resembling almost nobody in her own time. She does not compete with the male poets of the day, even with her brother, Dante Gabriel Rossetti. Influences on her were confined to the Bible and to English and Italian folklore. Yet her sensibility has a directness, a warmth and a passion for truth, which is essentially feminine. She is not a poet of width of experience or great range of interests, but she goes deep.

The Rossettis were a literary family. Christina and her sister and two brothers were three-quarters Italian in origin, and were brought up in a household still wrapped in Italian culture. Her father, Gabriele Rossetti, had been appointed Professor of Italian at King's College, London, after fleeing oppression in his native land at the hand of the Bourbons of Naples. Like many

Italian exiles in England – Foscolo and Alfieri, for instance – Rossetti was a fierce champion of liberty and an opponent of Catholic clericalism. Yet Christina's elder sister became a nun: an Anglican nun, since the children were brought up in the Church of England. The piety which possessed the girls eluded their brothers. Dante Gabriel's feeling for religion was all gilding and romantic attitudinizing. Her other brother, William, who was to be her editor and biographer, was more practical, though he too partook of the revolutionary artistic ethos of the Pre-Raphaelite brotherhood. The Italian half of Christina's mother's parentage resided in the family name, Polidori, which occurs also in the lives of Byron and Shelley.

Despite this Italianness, underlined by the endless comings and goings of Italian exiles at the Rossetti house, Christina's training, at her mother's hands, was in English literature and English piety. Nor is there anything Continental about the aims and aesthetic views of the Pre-Raphaelite brotherhood, other than its name. Languid, sensual, enervating, even consciously decadent on occasions, the Pre-Raphaelites were the most English of all artists. In their rejection of the prevailing tone of Victorianism, they became yet more representatively Victorian. Christina Rossetti was far removed in temperament from the romantic agonies of her brother, of Lizzie Siddell, William and Janey Morris and the Burne-Joneses, but she was as much a lover of detail and of intensity of atmosphere as any of them. Next to Tennyson, she had the best ear of her age. Every one of her poems falls on the reader's senses in an exquisite arrangement of sound. She is repetitive in subject matter – time, death, the seasons, lost love – but her poems work beautiful variations on this traditional material. Above all, she is the poet of daydreaming and longing for the peace and perfection of Paradise. She is a religious poet, but avoids all doctrine and threats.

Christina Rossetti's most famous single poem (an extract from which is included in this selection) is 'Goblin Market'. It is also the poem which made her reputation in her own time, getting her into print before the rest of the Pre-Raphaelites, in 1862. In many ways it is not representative, having a somewhat squashy, overwrought side to it. But it is definitely not a child's poem, being more of an allegory of sensuality, and quite as closely detailed as a painting by Millais or Holman Hunt. Christina's better style is purged of merely 'poetical' language: it is spare, beautifully composed and however dreamy, never inexact. She is also a brilliant handler of stanzas and rhymes.

She was born in London in 1830 and died there in 1894. Twice she might have married, but religious scruples and a retiring personality prevented her. She wrote about the visible changes of season in the English countryside, but she was essentially a city dweller. The prevailing sadness of her verse must reflect the disappointments of her life. But today, a century after her prime, her poetry stands up clearly with all the authority of its truthfulness and its technique. The quiet woman has merged into the established poet.

My Friend

Two days ago with dancing glancing hair,
    With living lips and eyes;
    Now pale, dumb, blind, she lies;
So pale, yet still so fair.

We have not left her yet, not yet alone;
    But soon must leave her where
    She will not miss our care,
Bone of our bone.

Weep not, O friends, we should not weep:
    Our friend of friends lies full of rest;
    No sorrow rankles in her breast,
Fallen fast asleep.

She sleeps below,
    She wakes and laughs above.
    To-day, as she walked, let us walk in love:
To-morrow follow so.

Seasons

In Springtime when the leaves are young,
Clear dewdrops gleam like jewels, hung
On boughs the fair birds roost among.

When Summer comes with sweet unrest,
Birds weary of their mother's breast,
And look abroad and leave the nest.

In Autumn ere the waters freeze,
The swallows fly across the seas:—
If we could fly away with these!

In Winter when the birds are gone,
The sun himself looks starved and wan,
And starved the snow he shines upon.

My Dream

Hear now a curious dream I dreamed last night,
Each word whereof is weighed and sifted truth.

I stood beside Euphrates while it swelled
Like overflowing Jordan in its youth.
It waxed and coloured sensibly to sight;
Till out of myriad pregnant waves there welled
Young crocodiles, a gaunt blunt-featured crew,
Fresh-hatched perhaps and daubed with birthday dew.
The rest if I should tell, I fear my friend,
My closest friend, would deem the facts untrue;
And therefore it were wisely left untold;
Yet if you will, why, hear it to the end.

Each crocodile was girt with massive gold
And polished stones that with their wearers grew:
But one there was who waxed beyond the rest,
Wore kinglier girdle and a kingly crown,
Whilst crowns and orbs and sceptres starred his
     breast.
All gleamed compact and green with scale on scale,
But special burnishment adorned his mail
And special terror weighed upon his frown;
His punier brethren quaked before his tail,
Broad as a rafter, potent as a flail.
So he grew lord and master of his kin:
But who shall tell the tale of all their woes?
An execrable appetite arose,
He battened on them, crunched, and sucked them in.

He knew no law, he feared no binding law,
But ground them with inexorable jaw.
The luscious fat distilled upon his chin,
Exuded from his nostrils and his eyes,
While still like hungry death he fed his maw;
Till, every minor crocodile being dead
And buried too, himself gorged to the full,
He slept with breath oppressed and unstrung claw.

Oh marvel passing strange which next I saw!
In sleep he dwindled to the common size,
And all the empire faded from his coat.
Then from far off a wingèd vessel came,
Swift as a swallow, subtle as a flame:
I know not what it bore of freight or host,
But white it was as an avenging ghost.
It levelled strong Euphrates in its course;
Supreme yet weightless as an idle mote
It seemed to tame the waters without force
Till not a murmur swelled or billow beat.
Lo, as the purple shadow swept the sands,
The prudent crocodile rose on his feet,
And shed appropriate tears and wrung his hands.
What can it mean? you ask. I answer not
For meaning, but myself must echo, What?
And tell it as I saw it on the spot.

Looking Forward

Sleep, let me sleep, for I am sick of care;
　　Sleep, let me sleep, for my pain wearies me.
Shut out the light; thicken the heavy air
With drowsy incense; let a distant stream
Of music lull me, languid as a dream,
　　Soft as the whisper of a summer sea.

Pluck me no rose that groweth on a thorn,
　　Nor myrtle white and cold as snow in June,
Fit for a virgin on her marriage morn:
But bring me poppies brimmed with sleepy death,
And ivy choking what it garlandeth,
　　And primroses that open to the moon.

Listen, the music swells into a song,
　　A simple song I loved in days of yore;
The echoes take it up and up along
The hills, and the wind blows it back again. —
Peace, peace, there is a memory in that strain
　　Of happy days that shall return no more.

Oh peace! your music wakeneth old thought,
　　But not old hope that made my life so sweet,
Only the longing that must end in nought.
Have patience with me, friends, a little while:
For soon, where you shall dance and sing and smile,
　　My quickened dust may blossom at your feet.

Sweet thought that I may yet live and grow green,
    That leaves may yet spring from the withered root,
And buds and flowers and berries half unseen.
Then, if you haply muse upon the past,
Say this: Poor child, she has her wish at last;
    Barren through life, but in death bearing fruit.

A Pause

They made the chamber sweet with flowers
        and leaves,
    And the bed sweet with flowers on which I lay;
    While my soul, love-bound, loitered on its way.
I did not hear the birds about the eaves,
Nor hear the reapers talk among the sheaves:
    Only my soul kept watch from day to day,
    My thirsty soul kept watch for one away:—
Perhaps he loves, I thought, remembers, grieves.
At length there came the step upon the stair,
    Upon the lock the old familiar hand:
Then first my spirit seemed to scent the air
    Of Paradise; then first the tardy sand
Of time ran golden; and I felt my hair
    Put on a glory, and my soul expand.

Amor Mundi

'Oh, where are you going with your lovelocks
        flowing,
    On the west wind blowing along this valley track?'
'The downhill path is easy, come with me an' it
        please ye,
    We shall escape the uphill by never turning back.'

So they two went together in glowing August weather,
    The honey-breathing heather lay to their left and
        right;
And dear she was to dote on, her swift feet seemed to
        float on
    The air like soft twin pigeons too sportive to alight.

'Oh, what is that in heaven where grey cloudflakes are
        seven,
    Where blackest clouds hang riven just at the rainy
        skirt?'
'Oh, that's a meteor sent us, a message dumb,
        portentous,
    An undecipher'd solemn signal of help or hurt.'

'Oh, what is that glides quickly where velvet flowers
        grow thickly,
    Their scent comes rich and sickly?' 'A scaled and
        hooded worm.'
'Oh, what's that in the hollow, so pale I quake to
        follow?'
    'Oh, that's a thin dead body, which awaits the
        eternal term.'

'Turn again, O my sweetest,–turn again, false and
    fleetest:
  This beaten way thou beatest I fear is hell's own
    track.'
'Nay, too steep for hill-mounting; nay, too late for
    cost counting:
  This downhill path is easy, but there's no turning
    back.'

In the Lane

When my love came home to me,
  Pleasant summer bringing,
Every tree was out in leaf,
  Every bird was singing.

There I met her in the lane
  By those waters gleamy,
Met her toward the fall of day,
  Warm and dear and dreamy.
Did I loiter in the lane?
  None was there to see me.

Only roses in the hedge,
  Lilies on the river,
Saw our greeting fast and fond,
  Counted gift and giver,
Saw me take her to my home,
  Take her home forever.

Goblin Market

Morning and evening
Maids heard the goblins cry:
'Come buy our orchard fruits,
Come buy, come buy:
Apples and quinces,
Lemons and oranges,
Plump unpecked cherries,
Melons and raspberries,
Bloom-down-cheeked peaches,
Swart-headed mulberries,
Wild free-born cranberries,
Crab-apples, dewberries,
Pine-apples, blackberries,
Apricots, strawberries;—
All ripe together
In summer weather,—
Morns that pass by,
Fair eves that fly;
Come buy, come buy:
Our grapes fresh from the vine,
Pomegranates full and fine,
Dates and sharp bullaces,
Rare pears and greengages,
Damsons and bilberries,
Taste them and try:
Currants and gooseberries,
Bright-fire-like barberries,
Figs to fill your mouth,

Citrons from the South,
Sweet to tongue and sound to eye;
Come buy, come buy.'

Evening by evening
Among the brookside rushes,
Laura bowed her head to hear,
Lizzie veiled her blushes:
Crouching close together
In the cooling weather,
With clasping arms and cautioning lips,
With tingling cheeks and finger tips.
'Lie close,' Laura said,
Pricking up her golden head:
'We must not look at goblin men,
We must not buy their fruits:
Who knows upon what soil they fed
Their hungry thirsty roots?'
'Come buy,' call the goblins
Hobbling down the glen.
'Oh,' cried Lizzie, 'Laura, Laura,
You should not peep at goblin men.'
Lizzie covered up her eyes,
Covered close lest they should look;
Laura reared her glossy head,
And whispered like the restless brook:
'Look, Lizzie, look, Lizzie,
Down the glen tramp little men.
One hauls a basket,
One bears a plate,

One lugs a golden dish
Of many pounds weight.
How fair the vine must grow
Whose grapes are so luscious;
How warm the wind must blow
Through those fruit bushes.'
'No,' said Lizzie: 'No, no, no;
Their offers should not charm us,
Their evil gifts would harm us.'
She thrust a dimpled finger
In each ear, shut eyes and ran:
Curious Laura chose to linger
Wondering at each merchant man.
One had a cat's face,
One whisked a tail,
One tramped at a rat's pace,
One crawled like a snail,
One like a wombat prowled obtuse and furry,
One like a ratel tumbled hurry skurry.
She heard a voice like voice of doves
Cooing all together:
They sounded kind and full of loves
In the pleasant weather.

Laura stretched her gleaming neck
Like a rush-imbedded swan,
Like a lily from the beck,
Like a moonlit poplar branch,
Like a vessel at the launch
When its last restraint is gone.

A Birthday

My heart is like a singing bird
  Whose nest is in a watered shoot:
My heart is like an apple-tree
  Whose boughs are bent with thickset fruit;
My heart is like a rainbow shell
  That paddles in a halcyon sea;
My heart is gladder than all these
  Because my love is come to me.

Raise me a dais of silk and down;
  Hang it with vair and purple dyes;
Carve it in doves and pomegranates,
  And peacocks with a hundred eyes;
Work it in gold and silver grapes,
  In leaves and silver fleurs-de-lys;
Because the birthday of my life
  Is come, my love is come to me.

Luscious and Sorrowful

Beautiful, tender, wasting away for sorrow;
Thus today; and how shall it be with thee tomorrow?
  Beautiful, tender—what else?
    A hope tells.

Beautiful, tender, keeping the jubilee
In the land of home together, past death and sea;
  No more change or death, no more
    Salt sea-shore.

Eve

'While I sit at the door,
Sick to gaze within,
Mine eye weepeth sore
For sorrow and sin:
As a tree my sin stands
To darken all lands;
Death is the fruit it bore.

'How have Eden bowers grown
Without Adam to bend them?
How have Eden flowers blown,
Squandering their sweet breath,
Without me to tend them?
The Tree of Life was ours,
Tree twelvefold-fruited,
Most lofty tree that flowers,
Most deeply rooted:
I chose the Tree of Death.

'Hadst thou but said me nay,
    Adam my brother,
I might have pined away—
    I, but none other:
God might have let thee stay
Safe in our garden,
By putting me away
Beyond all pardon.

'I, Eve, sad mother
Of all who must live,

I, not another,
Plucked bitterest fruit to give
My friend, husband, lover.
O wanton eyes, run over!
Who but I should grieve?
Cain hath slain his brother:
Of all who must die mother,
Miserable Eve!'

Thus she sat weeping,
Thus Eve our mother,
Where one lay sleeping
Slain by his brother.
Greatest and least
Each piteous beast
To hear her voice
Forgot his joys
And set aside his feast.

The mouse paused in his walk
And dropped his wheaten stalk;
Grave cattle wagged their heads
In rumination;
The eagle gave a cry
From his cloud station:
Larks on thyme beds
Forbore to mount or sing;
Bees drooped upon the wing;
The raven perched on high
Forgot his ration;
The conies in their rock,

A feeble nation,
Quaked sympathetical;
The mocking-bird left off to mock;
Huge camels knelt as if
In deprecation;
The kind hart's tears were falling;
Chattered the wistful stork;
Dove-voices with a dying fall
Cooed desolation,
Answering grief by grief.

Only the serpent in the dust,
Wriggling and crawling,
Grinned an evil grin and thrust
His tongue out with its fork.

Lines from
'What Good Shall My Life Do Me?'

Love in the gracious rain distils:
Love moves the subtle fountain-rills
To fertilize uplifted hills,

And seedful valleys fertilize:
Love stills the hungry lion's cries,
And the young raven satisfies:

Love hangs this earth in space: Love rolls
Fair worlds rejoicing on their poles,
And girds them round with aureoles:

Love lights the sun: Love through the dark
Lights the moon's evanescent arc:
Same Love lights up the glow-worm's spark:

Love rears the great: Love tends the small:
Breaks off the yoke, breaks down the wall:
Accepteth all, fulfilleth all.

O ye who taste that Love is sweet,
Set waymarks for the doubtful feet
That stumble on in search of it.

Sing hymns of Love, that those who hear
Far off in pain may lend an ear,
Rise up and wonder and draw near.

Lead lives of Love, that others who
Behold your lives may kindle too
With Love and cast their lots with you.

Up-hill

Does the road wind up-hill all the way?
  Yes, to the very end.
Will the day's journey take the whole long day?
  From morn to night, my friend.

But is there for the night a resting-place?
  A roof for when the slow dark hours begin.
May not the darkness hide it from my face?
  You cannot miss that inn.

Shall I meet other wayfarers at night?
  Those who have gone before.
Then must I knock, or call when just in sight?
  They will not keep you standing at that door.

Shall I find comfort, travel-sore and weak?
  Of labour you shall find the sum.
Will there be beds for me and all who seek?
  Yea, beds for all who come.

The Queen of Hearts

How comes it, Flora, that, whenever we
Play cards together, you invariably,
    However the pack parts,
    Still hold the Queen of Hearts?

I've scanned you with a scrutinizing gaze,
Resolved to father these your secret ways:
    But sift them as I will,
    Your ways are secret still.

I cut and shuffle; shuffle, cut, again;
But all my cutting, shuffling, proves in vain:
    Vain hope, vain forethought too;
    That Queen still falls to you.

I dropped her once, prepense; but, ere the deal
Was dealt, your instinct seemed her loss to feel:
    'There should be one card more,'
    You said, and searched the floor.

I cheated once; I made a private notch
In Heart-Queen's back, and kept a lynx-eyed watch;
    Yet such another back
    Deceived me in the pack:

The Queen of Clubs assumed by arts unknown
An imitative dint that seemed my own;
    This notch, not of my doing,
    Misled me to my ruin.

It baffles me to puzzle out the clue,
Which must be skill, or craft, or luck in you:
    Unless, indeed, it be
    Natural affinity.

Stanzas from 'Three Stages'

The fruitless thought of what I might have been,
    Haunting me ever, will not let me rest.
A cold North wind has withered all my green,
    My sun is in the West.

But, where my palace stood, with the same stone
    I will uprear a shady hermitage:
And there my spirit shall keep house alone,
    Accomplishing its age.

There other garden-beds shall lie around,
    Full of sweet-briar and incense-bearing thyme:
There will I sit, and listen for the sound
    Of the last lingering chime.

Echo

Come to me in the silence of the night;
  Come in the speaking silence of a dream:
Come with soft rounded cheeks and eyes as bright
    As sunlight on a stream;
      Come back in tears,
O memory, hope, love of finished years.

Oh dream how sweet, too sweet, too bitter sweet,
  Whose wakening should have been in Paradise,
Where souls brimfull of love abide and meet;
    Where thirsting longing eyes
      Watch the slow door
That opening, letting in, lets out no more.

Yet come to me in dreams, that I may live
  My very life again though cold in death:
Come back to me in dreams, that I may give
    Pulse for pulse, breath for breath:
      Speak low, lean low,
As long ago, my love, how long ago!

The Heart Knoweth Its Own Bitterness

When all the over-work of life
　　Is finished once, and fast asleep
We swerve no more beneath the knife
　　But taste that silence cool and deep;
Forgetful of the highways rough,
　　Forgetful of the thorny scourge,
　　Forgetful of the tossing surge,
Then shall we find it is enough?

How can we say 'enough' on earth—
　　'Enough' with such a craving heart?
I have not found it since my birth,
　　But still have bartered part for part.
I have not held and hugged the whole,
　　But paid the old to gain the new:
　　Much have I paid, yet much is due,
Till I am beggared sense and soul.

I used to labour, used to strive
　　For pleasure with a restless will:
Now if I save my soul alive
　　All else what matters, good or ill?
I used to dream alone, to plan
　　Unspoken hopes and days to come:—
　　Of all my past this is the sum—
I will not lean on child of man.

To give, to give, not to receive!
　　I long to pour myself, my soul,
Not to keep back or count or leave,

But king with king to give the whole.
I long for one to stir my deep—
    I have had enough of help and gift—
    I long for one to search and sift
Myself, to take myself and keep.

You scratch my surface with your pin,
    You stroke me smooth with hushing breath:—
Nay pierce, nay probe, nay dig within,
    Probe my quick core and sound my depth.
You call me with a puny call,
    You talk, you smile, you nothing do:
    How should I spend my heart on you,
My heart that so outweighs you all?

Your vessels are by much too strait:
    Were I to pour, you could not hold.—
Bear with me: I must bear to wait,
    A fountain sealed through heat and cold.
Bear with me days or months or years:
    Deep must call deep until the end
    When friend shall no more envy friend
Nor vex his friend at unawares.

Not in this world of hope deferred,
    This world of perishable stuff:—
Eye hath not seen nor ear hath heard
    Nor heart conceived that full 'enough':
Here moans the separating sea,
    Here harvests fail, here breaks the heart:
    There God shall join and no man part,
I full of Christ and Christ of me.

Pastime

A boat amid the ripples, drifting, rocking;
Two idle people, without pause or aim;
While in the ominous West there gathers darkness
    Flushed with flame.

A hay-cock in a hay-field, backing, lapping;
Two drowsy people pillowed round-about;
While in the ominous West across the darkness
    Flame leaps out.

Better a wrecked life than a life so aimless,
Better a wrecked life than a life so soft:
The ominous West glooms thundering, with its fire
    Lit aloft.

Somewhere or Other

Somewhere or other there must surely be
    The face not seen, the voice not heard,
The heart that not yet—never yet—ah me!
    Made answer to my word.

Somewhere or other, may be near or far;
    Past land and sea, clean out of sight;
Beyond the wandering moon, beyond the star
    That tracks her night by night.

Somewhere or other, may be far or near;
    With just a wall, a hedge, between;
With just the last leaves of the dying year
    Fallen on a turf grown green.

Memory

1

I nursed it in my bosom while it lived,
  I hid it in my heart when it was dead.
In joy I sat alone; even so I grieved
    Alone, and nothing said.

I shut the door to face the naked truth,
  I stood alone–I faced the truth alone,
Stripped bare of self-regard or forms or ruth
    Till first and last were shown.

I took the perfect balances and weighed;
  No shaking of my hand disturbed the poise;
Weighed, found it wanting: not a word I said,
    But silent made my choice.

None know the choice I made; I make it still.
  None know the choice I made and broke my heart,
Breaking mine idol: I have braced my will
    Once, chosen for once my part.

I broke it at a blow, I laid it cold,
  Crushed in my deep heart where it used to live.
My heart dies inch by inch; the time grows old,
    Grows old in which I grieve.

2

I have a room whereinto no one enters
   Save I myself alone:
   There sits a blessed memory on a throne,
There my life centres;

While winter comes and goes–oh tedious comer!–
   And while its nip-wind blows;
   While bloom the bloodless lily and warm rose
Of lavish summer.

If any should force entrance he might see there
   One buried yet not dead,
   Before whose face I no more bow my head
Or bend my knee there;

But often in my worn life's autumn weather
   I watch there with clear eyes,
   And think how it will be in Paradise
When we're together.

L.E.L.

'Whose heart was breaking for a little love.'

Downstairs I laugh, I sport and jest with all;
    But in my solitary room above
I turn my face in silence to the wall;
    My heart is breaking for a little love.
        Though winter frosts are done,
        And birds pair every one,
And leaves peep out, for springtide is begun.

I feel no spring, while spring is well-nigh blown,
    I find no nest, while nests are in the grove:
Woe's me for mine own heart that dwells alone,
    My heart that breaketh for a little love.
        While golden in the sun
        Rivulets rise and run,
While lilies bud, for springtide is begun.

All love, are loved, save only I; their hearts
    Beat warm with love and joy, beat full thereof:
They cannot guess, who play the pleasant parts,
    My heart is breaking for a little love.
        While bee-hives wake and whirr,
        And rabbit thins his fur,
In living spring that sets the world astir.

I deck myself with silks and jewelry,
    I plume myself like any mated dove:
They praise my rustling show, and never see
    My heart is breaking for a little love.

While sprouts green lavender
With rosemary and myrrh,
For in quick spring the sap is all astir.

Perhaps some saints in glory guess the truth,
Perhaps some angels read it as they move,
And cry one to another full of ruth,
'Her heart is breaking for a little love.'
Though other things have birth,
And leap and sing for mirth,
When springtime wakes and clothes and feeds the
earth.

Yet saith a saint, 'Take patience for thy scathe';
Yet saith an angel: 'Wait, and thou shalt prove
True best is last, true life is born of death,
O thou, heart-broken for a little love.
Then love shall fill thy girth,
And love make fat thy dearth,
When new spring builds new heaven and clean new
earth.'

A Triad

Three sang of love together: one with lips
   Crimson, with cheeks and bosom in a glow,
Flushed to the yellow hair and finger-tips;
   And one there sang who soft and smooth as snow
   Bloomed like a tinted hyacinth at a show;
And one was blue with famine after love,
   Who like a harpstring snapped rang harsh and low
The burden of what those were singing of.
One shamed herself in love; one temperately
   Grew gross in soulless love, a sluggish wife;
One famished died for love. Thus two of three
   Took death for love and won him after strife;
One droned in sweetness like a fattened bee:
   All on the threshold, yet all short of life.

A Christmas Carol

In the bleak mid-winter
   Frosty wind made moan,
Earth stood hard as iron,
   Water like a stone;
Snow had fallen, snow on snow,
   Snow on snow,
In the bleak mid-winter
   Long ago.

Our God, Heaven cannot hold Him
   Nor earth sustain;
Heaven and earth shall flee away
   When he comes to reign:
In the bleak mid-winter
   A stable-place sufficed
The Lord God Almighty
   Jesus Christ.

Enough for Him, whom cherubim
   Worship night and day,
A breastful of milk
   And a mangerful of hay;
Enough for Him, whom angels
   Fall down before,
The ox and ass and camel
   Which adore.

Angels and archangels
    May have gathered there,
Cherubim and seraphim
    Thronged the air;
But only His mother
    In her maiden bliss
Worshipped the Beloved
    With a kiss.

What can I give Him,
    Poor as I am?
If I were a shepherd
    I would bring a lamb,
If I were a Wise Man
    I would do my part,—
Yet what I can I give Him,
    Give my heart.

Mary Magdalene

She came in deep repentance,
  And knelt down at His feet
Who can change the sorrow into joy,
  The bitter into sweet.

She had cast away her jewels
  And her rich attire,
And her breast was filled with a holy shame,
  And her heart with a holy fire.

Her tears were more precious
  Than her precious pearls—
Her tears that fell upon His feet
  As she wiped them with her curls.

Her youth and her beauty
  Were budding to their prime;
But she wept for the great transgression,
  The sin of other time.

Trembling betwixt hope and fear,
  She sought the King of Heaven,
Forsook the evil of her ways,
  Loved much, and was forgiven.

Twilight Calm

Oh pleasant eventide!
Clouds on the western side
Grow grey and greyer, hiding the warm sun:
The bees and birds, their happy labours done,
    Seek their close nests and bide.

Screened in the leafy wood
The stock-doves sit and brood:
The very squirrel leaps from bough to bough
But lazily; pauses; and settles now
    Where once he stored his food.

One by one the flowers close,
Lily and dewy rose
Shutting their tender petals from the moon:
The grasshoppers are still; but not so soon
    Are still the noisy crows.

The dormouse squats and eats
Choice little dainty bits
Beneath the spreading roots of a broad lime;
Nibbling his fill he stops from time to time
    And listens where he sits.

From far the lowings come
Of cattle driven home:
From farther still the wind brings fitfully
The vast continual murmur of the sea,
    Now loud, now almost dumb.

The gnats whirl in the air,
The evening gnats; and there
The owl opes broad his eyes and wings to sail
For prey; the bat wakes; and the shell-less snail
Comes forth, clammy and bare.

Hark! that's the nightingale,
Telling the self-same tale
Her song told when this ancient earth was young:
So echoes answered when her song was sung
In the first wooded vale.

We call it love and pain,
The passion of her strain;
And yet we little understand or know:
Why should it not be rather joy that so
Throbs in each throbbing vein?

In separate herds the deer
Lie; here the bucks, and here
The does, and by its mother sleeps the fawn:
Through all the hours of night until the dawn
They sleep, forgetting fear.

The hare sleeps where it lies,
With wary half-closed eyes;
The cock has ceased to crow, the hen to cluck:
Only the fox is out, some heedless duck
Or chicken to surprise.

Remote, each single star
Comes out, till there they are
All shining brightly. How the dews fall damp!
While close at hand the glow-worm lights her lamp,
Or twinkles from afar.

But evening now is done
As much as if the sun
Day-giving had arisen in the East—
For night has come; and the great calm has ceased,
The quiet sands have run.

Song

When I am dead, my dearest,
  Sing no sad songs for me;
Plant thou no roses at my head,
  Nor shady cypress tree:
Be the green grass above me
  With showers and dewdrops wet:
And if thou wilt, remember,
  And if thou wilt, forget.

I shall not see the shadows,
  I shall not feel the rain;
I shall not hear the nightingale
  Sing on as if in pain:
And dreaming through the twilight
  That doth not rise nor set,
Haply I may remember,
  And haply may forget.

NOTES ON THE PICTURES

p. 122 Walter Crane (1845–1915). *Madonna Lilies in a Garden*, 1908. Oil on canvas.
Private Collection. Photo: Bridgeman Art Library, London.

p. 129 Frederick Walker (1840–75). *Spring*, 1864. Watercolour.
Reproduced by courtesy of the Board of Trustees of the Victoria and Albert Museum, London.

p. 132 Dante Gabriel Rossetti (1828–82). *Beata Beatrix*, 1864–70. Oil on canvas.
Reproduced by permission of the Trustees of the Tate Gallery, London.

p. 137 Frederick Smallfield (1829–1915). *Early Lovers*, 1858. Oil on canvas.
Reproduced by permission of City of Manchester Art Galleries.

p. 140 Arthur Rackham (1867–1939). *White and Golden Lizzie Stood*. Book illustration from an edition of *Goblin Market*, 1933.
© Harrap Ltd, London.

p. 145 J. R. Spencer Stanhope (1829–1908). *Eve Tempted*, exhibited 1877. Tempera on panel.
Reproduced by permission of City of Manchester Art Galleries.

p. 149 Edward Burne-Jones (1833–98). *Ladder of Heaven*, 1882–98. Watercolour.
Reproduced by permission of the Trustees of the British Museum, London.

p. 152 Francis Danby (1793–1861). *Disappointed Love*, exhibited 1821. Oil on panel.
Reproduced by courtesy of the Board of Trustees of the Victoria and Albert Museum, London.

p. 157 Dante Gabriel Rossetti. *Reverie*, 1868. Coloured chalks.
Reproduced by courtesy of Christie's, London. Photo: Bridgeman Art Library, London.

p. 160 Richard Redgrave (1804–88). *The Governess*, 1844. Oil on canvas.
Reproduced by courtesy of the Board of Trustees of the Victoria and Albert Museum, London.

p. 165 Alexander Mann (1853–1908). *The New Baby*, c. 1886–8. Oil on canvas.
Reproduced by courtesy of The Fine Art Society, London.

p. 169 William J. Webbe (*fl.* 1853–78). *Twilight*, date unknown. Oil on canvas.
Private collection. Photo: Bridgeman Art Library, London.

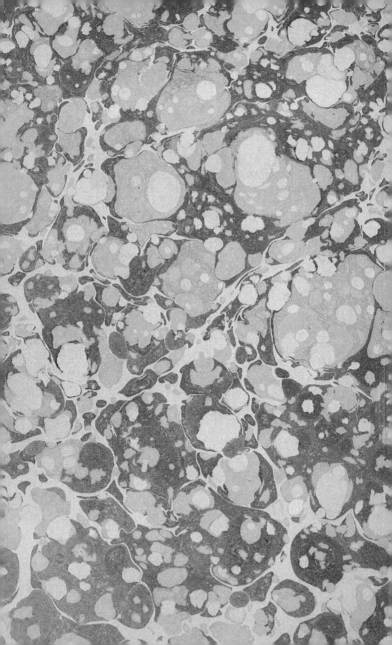